A LITTLE BOOK

of SELF-CARE

for THOSE

WHO GRIEVE

A LITTLE BOOK

of SELF-CARE

for THOSE

WHO GRIEVE

PAULA BECKER

with illustrations by
REBEKAH NICHOLS

GIRL FRIDAY BOOKS

 GIRL FRIDAY BOOKS

Published by Girl Friday Books™, Seattle

Produced by Girl Friday Productions
www.girlfridayproductions.com

Design: Rachel Marek
Development & editorial: Sara Spees Addicott
Production editorial: Dave Valencia

Cover image, title page, and pages 13, 22, 35, 39, 48,
56, 75, 76: © Suto Norbert Zsolt/Shutterstock

ISBN (hardcover): 978-1-7363579-5-8
ISBN (e-book): 978-1-7363579-6-5
ISBN (audio): 978-1-954854-10-9
Library of Congress Control Number: 2021904040

First edition

PREFACE

On June 29, 2017, my twenty-five-year-old son, Hunter, was killed.

The shock of Hunter's death instantly deadened me. I curled into the couch corner, moving little. When movement became inescapable, my body pressed thickly through what was now an unfamiliar landscape. I had no appetite but could not quench my thirst. I had, at first, little information. My thoughts skittered randomly, unable to form a pattern. Days and nights were marked by how many of them had passed since Hunter's death.

Eventually, I blindly reached for books to help me understand how to navigate the grief engulfing me. I did find books, but they were too wordy for my shattered attention span. Too big to carry easily, to be a touchstone. I wanted a guide: short, prescriptive, realistic. A book to help me help myself, to help me live within my new bereaved reality.

A Little Book of Self-Care for Those Who Grieve began as notes scratched out over many midnights, thoughts formed as I lay sleepless or in the aftermath of painful dreams. This book aims to be a hand to hold for others who are grieving. Reader, it is for your support. Use this book however you want to. Read it straight through, or read a page a day. Turn to it when you need to. I hope its words will lift and carry those who read them, as surely as the grieving reader carries the book.

A LITTLE BOOK

of SELF-CARE

for THOSE

WHO GRIEVE

Someone is gone,

and they will not come back.

Weep.

Scream.

Hate.

Disbelieve.

Go numb.

Breathe.

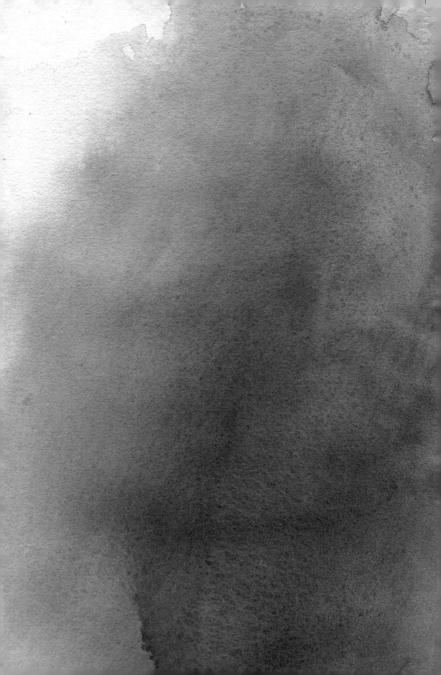

Rage.

Breathe.

Curse God (or gods).

Beg God (or gods).

Breathe.

Remember.

Feel it, what you feel.

Let it be.

Sit with it, because you have no choice.

Sit with it. Let it be.

This is the only work:

breathe.

Add lemon to your water.

Sip.

Eat something if you can.

A little is okay.

There is no right or wrong way to feel.

There is just how you feel.

Feel.

Breathe.

Be kind, now. Kind to you.

Grief hurts in every way. It hurts your body.

Sometimes sensation comforts when words cannot:

Water against skin as you stroke through.

The weighty quilt, more frayed than whole, your great-grandmother pieced decades ago.

Mug, hot from tea.

Bowl, warm from soup.

Comfort food is what someone else made that you can eat. Also, the echo of those dishes, which you may re-create: watermelon/feta/mint salad, even out of season. Lentil soup. Baked rigatoni, tucked in the fridge, consumed by spoonful rather than bowlful.

Eating nothing else is fine. Eating these same meals for weeks, months, years is fine. Anything that warms or cools or comforts, any time, for any length of time, is fine. Maybe what matters isn't the specific food. Maybe it's that receiving it makes us feel cherished.

Not everyone has been initiated into grief. Friends may not know what to say. Your grief may frighten them. This is okay. Their fear is not your work. Your work is you.

You are accident-prone.
Be extra careful.

Whether you realize it or
not, you are in shock.

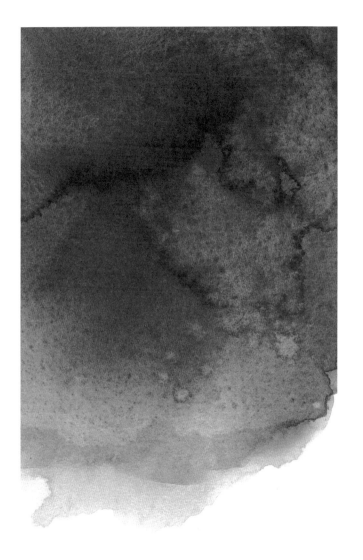

If you can manage it, try not to drive. Grief wells and overflows in the car's safe space. Can someone drive you? Can you call for a ride? If you must drive, take a five-minute grief meditation before you start the car. Focus. Breathe, as best you can. Practice staying present behind the wheel.

If you panic (and you may), pull over. If images arise (they may), just breathe. Relax your muscles. Take time. (It will take time.) Breathe.

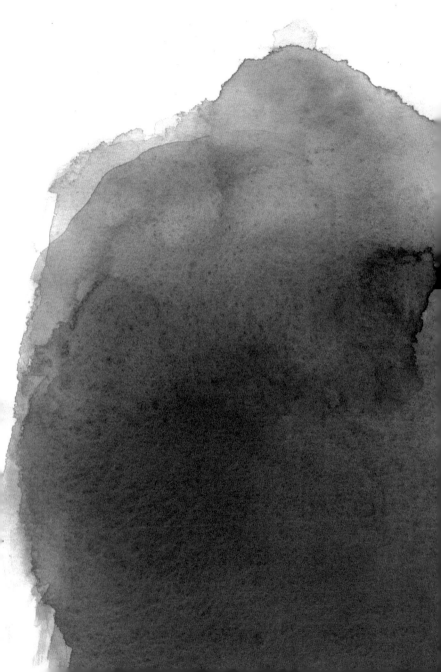

Preserve what energy you have. Delegate. Try to tell people what you need, specifically, if you know. If you don't know what you need, that's okay too. Do what you want to do, if anything. Hand other tasks away, if that feels right.

Time may feel strange: unreal, or hyperreal.

Tasks will present themselves.

Plan his memorial.

Write her death notice.

These may seem monumental, impossible. They may seem like a precious chance.

Plan what you can, if that feels right. Ask for help, if help is what you need.

Friends, family gather:

A flock of angels supporting you,

remembering the one you've lost—who they have also lost.

In church, at park, by gravesite, over the internet:

Their presence may be physical or virtual,

but it is real.

Mourn, rely.

Retell, remember.

Maybe the gathering does not fit what you planned. Someone important to you doesn't come. Someone says something that feels wrong to you. Your grief has made you raw, shortened your patience. Being confronted—again—with the reality that you control so little may feel especially cruel now.

Notice your disappointment, your rawness. These things are.

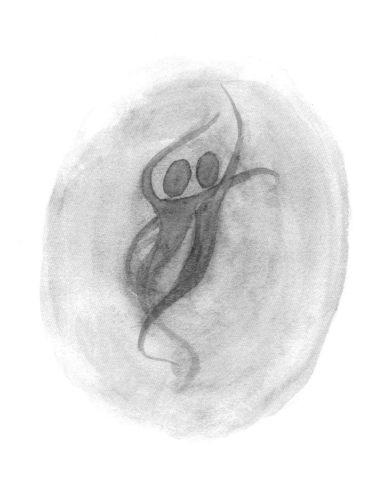

You may ask yourself, *When will this end? How do I do this?*

Your grief will teach you, over time. That is hard to hear. Grief is a lifelong process, a new relationship. The way you and your grief interact—your dance with grief—will change over time. Your grief will take the lead and be a bumpy partner. After a while, you will learn one another's rhythm. There may even be fleeting moments where pain holds grace.

You may be grieving someone who was hard to love, or with whom intimacy was challenging. This will shape your grief. There is nothing wrong with you. Relationships in life shape grief itself. Relationships are a joint project that begins in life and continues after death. Think of what you still need to say to the one you've lost. You may need to express anger or disappointment. This is okay. Say what you need to say, silently or out loud, if that feels right.

If your loved one was ravaged by disease, it may take time for you to remember their wholeness. If your loved one died suddenly, you may grieve the theft of a last goodbye.

Make a safe space, a blanket fort.

Give yourself what you need (as long as doing it won't harm you).

Stay in bed. Listen.

Allow yourself to hear, when

what your body tells you it needs

changes.

Sleep (or not).

Breathe.

Give visible expression to your
grief. Cocoon yourself within
whatever comforts:

His bathrobe.

Her shirt.

That hand-knit shawl.

Sometimes it helps to wear the same clothes every day: less to decide that way, and something constant and familiar. Allow yourself.

Think magically, if that helps. Crystals, stones, runes.

Labradorite, lava rock.

Rose quartz, yellow jasper.

You may feel your person's presence. Let them be there, if that feels right.

You may find comfort in the thought that your person is busy elsewhere. Let them be busy in their new reality, if that feels right. You have permission to find comfort in whatever thoughts bring comfort, whether you've thought that way before or not.

Rest in nature, or at
least in water. The sea,
the pool, the bath.

Tell and retell the story,
to claim it over time.
To make it real.

Write about it, if that helps. Fragments of dreams, thoughts you wish you could share.

Talk to the one you've lost, if that feels natural. What would the lost one say to you right now? What would you answer?

If you have ashes, take time
with them. Keep them
nearby as long as you want.

Say, try to say, goodbye.

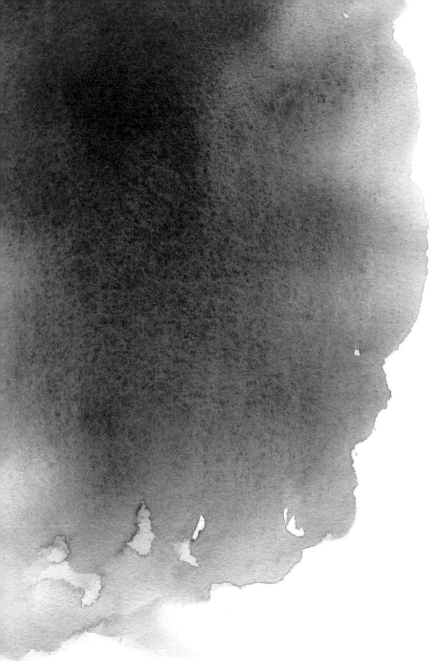

Tears, now, are clearing, venting.
Let them flow. Let your face
reflect your inner landscape.

The only way out of
this broken place is through.

Breathe. Hydrate. Nourish.

Breathe.

Mindful grieving is what comes next, maybe forever.

Mourning is active. Grief is active. Move through grief, and let it move through you.

Dreams come. Let them out. Write them down. Hold them close. Your dreams may feel like visits from the one you've lost. She may seem real. His voice may sound just the way it once did.

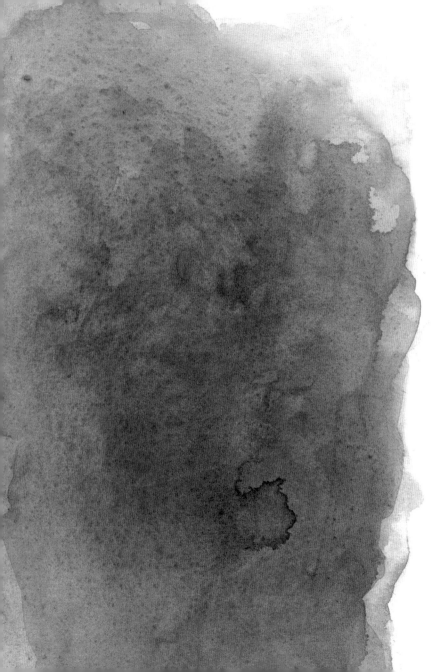

Journal, if it helps. Vent, remember, mourn. Ask questions that might not have answers. Sift through memories. Ponder, validate, claim.

Wash and anoint.

Let bathwater surround you, let
showers absolve you of the dust of grief.

Essential oils offer silent comfort,
asking nothing in return.

Palo Santo. Clary sage. Melissa.
Rose Absolute.

Can you be touched? Healing touch can help you process, can integrate this new reality. Massage lets trusted hands soothe, nurture. Touch can release. Touch can console. Touch can help patch the pain, help mend some of the damage grief does to the physical body.

Shock may be wearing off. Pain fills the void, along with memories of the one you've lost. Now what, you ask? More pain? But for how long? Your loss is permanent. You may feel that more fully now.

Move your grief, if that feels right. Sometimes physical exertion can bring a different kind of exhaustion, a small respite from the exhaustion of grief. Walk with friends who support you best. Walk alone in meditation. Move in whatever way feels helpful. Let movement temporarily vent the pressure weighing on you. Concentrate on the good medicine of air brushing your skin. Know that some things remain the same, even after enormous loss.

Consider yoga. Practice sitting with what cannot change, accepting what cannot be altered. Cry in savasana, also called corpse pose. Curl inward, face down, in child's pose. Rest. Let the ground hold you up.

Light candles. Name your loss. Take ancient comfort from the tiny flame, still bright in all the dark, still constant. Permit yourself to feel this tiny respite.

Allowing yourself to experience comfort is not a betrayal of the one you've lost.

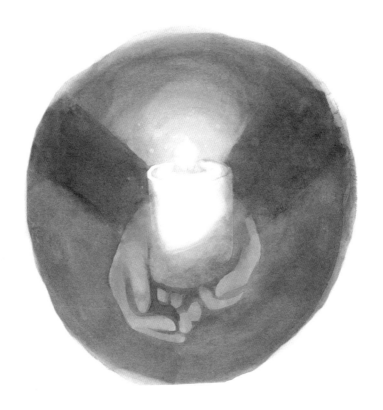

Consider poetry. Poetry can crack grief open and smooth it down, howl its depths, name its nuance.

And naming something is powerful old magic.

Ask friends for help when you are over-whelmed. Do not set time limits for yourself. If grief flares suddenly, as grief will do, cancel plans, even at the last minute.

Grief carves a new geography—
map this world. Old places can give
comfort. New places—even a grave—
can tether us, connect us to the one
we love.

Losing someone dear can shuffle friendships and family alliances. Relationships will change. Let them change, even if this is painful, another loss. This change is sometimes necessary. It can bring new opportunity, deepen insight.

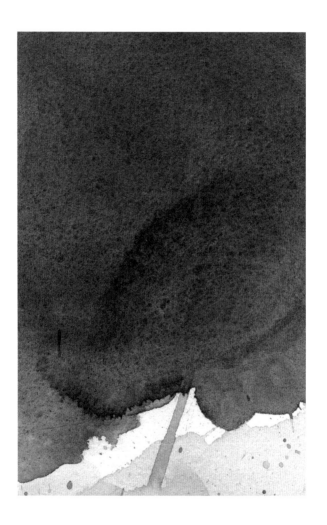

Compose a letter to the one you've lost, if that feels right. What do you need to say to them? What do you need them to tell you? Your conversations may change as your dance with grief changes you. Let them change. Let them grow.

All religions offer traditions
that may comfort and honor.
If it helps, use them, and
those whose ministry it is
to support and guide.

Continue retelling your story: to friends and family, to a grief group, maybe with a counselor or therapist. There is no privilege in unexpressed grief. Sharing helps carry it.

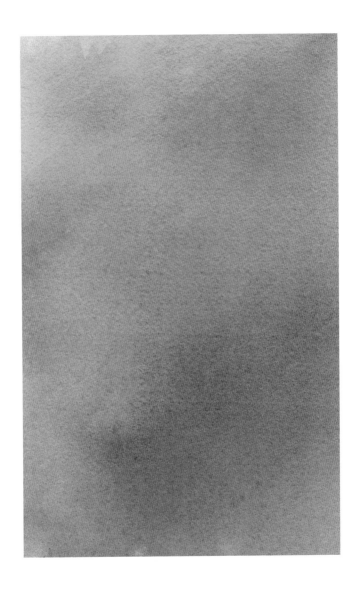

First days, first weeks, first months, first year will pass. Commemorations can help structure these hard times. Rituals can ease the path through anniversaries. Memorial tattoos, visiting places where your loved one feels close. Eat his favorite food. Walk through that park she loved. See what helps. You can change rituals from year to year, or not. The rituals belong to you.

Find a ring or necklace that sings your person's story. Wear it all the time, letting the stone, the silver, whisper that story to you constantly. Let it be private, or public. A secret, or a badge.

Wear, carry, cradle, breathe your person's clothing, if you have it. His favorite shirt, the robe she wore are now transitional and sacred objects. Relics. Surround yourself with them, if that helps.

Build an altar of remembrance, a shrine: a stone, a photograph, a childhood toy. Crystal, feather, pack of cigarettes. Tiny coffee cup, refilled each day. Offerings that bind you to the one you've lost, tether that life. Let altar be umbilicus, feeding both ways, grief communing with spirit, physical objects begging that spirit not to stray. Later, perhaps, or maybe never, let altar be a place that holds that deep connection, freeing you just a little. Allowing you to move through days.

All this advice will pale in the stark agony of your grief. None of these words will be enough. What helps is different for everyone, and may change over time.

Some days will be less bad. Let them be less bad. On these days, allow yourself to notice what is good, taste what is sweet, recognize relief.

Some days will be extraordinarily hard, even years after your loss. Eventually, pain and joy will coexist. Neither will banish the other.

Let all days be, the good days and the bad. Notice them. Feel them. Let them be.

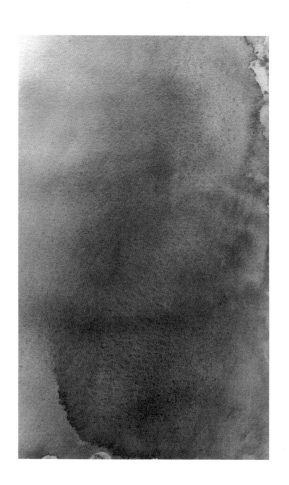

Grief changes us. Grief is a new companion. You will never be exactly who you were before your bereavement. No one can promise you it will get better. Over a long time, it will get different. Different doesn't mean forgetting the one you've lost, or betraying them. Different means reengaging in the world. Let that happen, as that begins to slowly start to seem right.

Know that we all,
in time, walk this road.

We sit with loss. We recognize it.
We sit with grief. We feel it. We feel it.

Breathe.

RESOURCES FOR THOSE WHO GRIEVE

WEBSITES

Camp Widow campwidow.org

Modern Loss modernloss.com

Refuge in Grief refugeingrief.com

The Compassionate Friends compassionatefriends.org

What's Your Grief? whatsyourgrief.com

PODCAST

Grief Out Loud www.dougy.org/news-media/podcasts

B O O K S

Poetry:

Kevin Young, ed., *The Art of Losing: Poems of Grief and Healing* (New York: Bloomsbury, 2013)

Therapeutic:

Megan Devine, *It's OK That You're Not OK: Meeting Grief and Loss in a Culture That Doesn't Understand* (Boulder, CO: Sounds True, 2017)

Karla Helbert, *Yoga for Grief and Loss* (London: Singing Dragon, 2015)

Antonio Sausys, *Yoga for Grief Relief: Simple Practices for Transforming Your Grieving Mind & Body* (Oakland, CA: New Harbinger Publications, 2014)

Memoir:

Joan Didion, *The Year of Magical Thinking* (New York: Knopf, 2005)

Danielle Geller, *Dog Flowers* (New York: One World, 2021)

Jayson Greene, *Once More We Saw Stars: A Memoir of Life and Love After Unimaginable Loss* (New York: Knopf, 2019)

Kate Inglis, *Notes for the Everlost: A Field Guide to Grief* (Boulder, CO: Shambhala, 2018)

Leslie Gray Streeter, *Black Widow: A Sad-Funny Journey Through Grief for People Who Normally Avoid Books with Words Like "Journey" in the Title* (New York: Little, Brown and Company, 2020)

Fiction:

Max Porter, *Grief Is the Thing with Feathers* (Minneapolis: Graywolf Press, 2016)

For Children:

Bryan Mellonie and Robert Ingpen, *Lifetimes: The beautiful way to explain death to children* (New York: Bantam, 1983)

Pat Schwiebert and Chuck DeKlyen, *Tear Soup: A Recipe for Healing After Loss* (Portland, OR: Grief Watch, 1999)

A C K N O W L E D G M E N T S

Thanks to Barry Brown, Sawyer Brown, and Lillie Brown, with all my love.

To Laura Takacs, my deepest gratitude.

Thanks to Juliana Aldous, Karen Maeda Allman, Claire Andersen, Elinor Appel, Andrew Berzanskis, Amy Caldwell, Abigail Carter, Elizabeth Chaison, Jodee Fenton, Heather Henderson, Lisa Hensell, Priscilla Long, and Melissa Shaffer.

Many thanks to the amazing team at Girl Friday Books, especially Ingrid Emerick, Sara Spees Addicott, Kristin Mehus-Roe, and Leah Tracosas Jenness.

In memory of Hunter Maxwell Becker Brown, always.

ABOUT THE AUTHOR
AND ILLUSTRATOR

PAULA BECKER is the author of *A House on Stilts: Mothering in the Age of Opioid Addiction*, *Looking For Betty MacDonald: The Egg, The Plague, Mrs. Piggle-Wiggle and I*, and coauthor of *The Future Remembered: The 1962 Seattle World's Fair and Its Legacy* and *Alaska-Yukon-Pacific Exposition: Washington's First World's Fair*. More than three hundred of Paula's essays documenting all aspects of Washington state's history appear on HistoryLink.org. She lives in Seattle.

REBEKAH NICHOLS is an artist who works primarily in watercolor and has worked as an illustrator for several years. She has done work ranging from editorial to packaging. She graduated from the University of Kansas with a BFA in Design with a concentration in Illustration in 2007. She lives in Austin, Texas.